SANDS
OF THE WELL

Books by Denise Levertov

Poetry

The Double Image
Here and Now
Overland to the Islands
With Eyes at the Back of Our Heads
The Jacob's Ladder
O Taste and See
The Sorrow Dance
Relearning the Alphabet
To Stay Alive
Footprints
The Freeing of the Dust
Life in the Forest
Collected Earlier Poems 1940–1960
Candles in Babylon
Poems 1960–1967
Oblique Prayers
Poems 1968–1972
Breathing the Water
A Door in the Hive
Evening Train
Sands of the Well

Prose

Poet in the World
Light Up the Cave
New & Selected Essays
Tesserae

Translations

Guillevic/Selected Poems
Joubert/Black Iris (Copper Canyon Press)

DENISE
LEVERTOV
❦

SANDS
OF THE WELL

A NEW DIRECTIONS BOOK

Grateful acknowledgment is made to the editors and publishers of magazines in which some of the poems in this collection first appeared: *American Poetry Review, Amicus Journal, Beloit Poetry Journal, Carolina Quarterly, Cat's Ear, Colorado Review, Connecticut Quarterly, Equinox, Image, Notre Dame Review, Poetry Ireland Review, Seneca, Sycamore,* and *Wilderness Review.*

Manufactured in the United States of America
New Directions Books are printed on acid-free paper
First published clothbound in 1996
Published simultaneously in Canada by Penguin Books Canada Limited

Library of Congress Cataloging-in-Publication Data
Levertov, Denise, 1923-
    Sands of the well / Denise Levertov.
      p. cm.
    ISBN 0–8112–1316–1 (alk. paper)
    I. Title.
    PS3562.E8876S26   1996   96–4324
    811'.54—dc20   CIP

Celebrating 60 years of publishing
for James Laughlin
by New Directions Publishing Corporation,
80 Eighth Avenue, New York 10011

Contents

I
Crow Spring

What Harbinger?

Glitter of grey
oarstrokes over
the waveless, dark,
secretive water.
A boat is moving
toward me
slowly, but who
is rowing and what
it brings I can't
yet see.

I spent the entire night leading a blind man
through an immense museum
so that (by internal bridges, or tunnels?
somehow!) he could avoid the streets,
the most dangerous avenues, all the swift
chaotic traffic . . .   I persuaded him
to allow my guidance, through to the other
distant doors, though once inside, labyrinthine corridors,
steps, jutting chests and chairs and stone arches
bewildered him as I named them at each swerve,
and were hard for me to manoeuver him
around and between. As he could perceive nothing,
I too saw only the obstacles, the objects
with sharp corners; not one painting, not one carved
credenza or limestone martyr.   We did at last
emerge, however, into that part of the city
he had been headed for when I took over;
he raised his hat in farewell, and went on, uphill,
tapping his stick. I stood looking after him,
watching as the street enfolded him, wondering
if he would make it, and after I woke, wondering still
what in me he was, and who
the *I* was that took that long short-cut with him
through room after room of beauty his blindness
hid from me as if it had never been.

You can live for years next door
to a big pinetree, honored to have
so venerable a neighbor, even
when it sheds needles all over your flowers
or wakes you, dropping big cones
onto your deck at still of night.
Only when, before dawn one year
at the vernal equinox, the wind
rises and rises, raising images
of cockleshell boats tossed among huge
advancing walls of waves,
do you become aware that always,
under respect, under your faith
in the pinetree's beauty, there lies
the fear it will crash some day
down on your house, on you in your bed,
on the fragility of the safe
dailiness you have almost
grown used to.

A sunset of such aqueous hints, subdued
opaline gleamings, so much grey among its
wan folds, fading
tangerine roses;
                    and in a rosetree—not a rosetree,
                    a young tree of some other species
                    which has become the noble
                    support, patient, perhaps eager,
                    of a capricious Gloire de Dijon—
          in this green
symbiosis of elder and wildening
rose, the evening wind is pulsing,
and the sound nearby
of a saxophone, slowly wistful
without being strictly sad.

For the first time, the certainty of return
to this imprinted scene, unchanging but for the height
of green thicket, rising year by year
beyond the cobwebbed windowpanes,
can not be assumed.

The Wound

My tree
had a secret wound.
Not lethal. And it was young.
But one withered branch
hung down.

When distant ocean's big V of silver
reaches straight up, rearing
between the hills that hold it,
don't you feel you could go and go
swift as hurricane till you
flung yourself at its wall, its
blue wall of spider silver,
and passed like Alice
into the blind mirror?

Wondering

*"The very act of lighting
the candle is prayer."*
Bro. David Steindl-Rast

Just to light the candle,
just to draw the breath
of a sigh towards the match,
is an act?
        A prayer?

Can it bridge the gulf
between our sense of being—
node, synapse, locus of hidden counsels
—and the multitudinous force of
world?

Some days, some moments
shiver in extreme fragility.
A trembling brittleness
of oak and iron. Splinterings, glassy shatterings,
threaten.
Evaporations of granite.
These are the danger moments:

different from fear of what we do, have done,
may do. Different from apprehension
of mortality, the closing cadence
of lived phrases, a continuum.

These are outside the pattern.

You've heard the way infant and ancient sleepers
stop sometimes between
one breath and the next?
You know the terror
of watching them.
It's like that.

As if the world were a thought
God was thinking and then
not thinking. Divine attention
turned away. Will breath and thought
resume?
       They do, for now.

In the night foundations crumble.
God's image was contrived
of beaten alloy. A thin clatter
as it tumbles from its niche.

Parts of your body ache,
each separate, ominous,
linked only by emplacement within
a worn skin. Convictions

wheel and scatter,
white birds affrighted.

In time you sleep. But wake
to the same sensation: adrift
mid-ocean, frayed mooring ropes
trailing behind you, swirling.

Yet when you open
unwilling eyes, you see the day
is sunlit. You walk
down to the real shore.

Over the city,
a scum of brown. But it is quiet
among the trees, grass
strewn with first-fallen leaves,
a sheen of dew. The past night

remains with you, but your attention
is drawn away from it
to taste the autumn light, falling
into your empty hands.

In each mind, even the most candid,
there are forests, where needled haze overshadows
the slippery duff and patches of snow long-frozen,
or else where mangroves, proliferant, vine-entwisted,
loom over warm mud that slowly bubbles.
In these forests there live certain events, shards
of memory, scraps of once-heard lore, intimations
once familiar—some painful, shameful, some
drably or laughably inconsequent, others
thoughts that the thinker
could never hold fast and begin to tell.
And some—a few—that are noble, tender,
and so complete in themselves, they had
no need of saying.
                There they dwell,
no sky above them, resting
like dragonflies on the dense air, or nested
on inaccessible twigs.
It is right that there are these secrets
(even the weightless ones have perhaps
some part to play in the unperceiveable whole)
and these forests; privacies
and the deep terrain to receive them.
Right that they rise at times into our ken,
and are acknowledged.

Rain and the dark. The owl,
terror of those he must hunt,
flies back and forth, hungry.
Darkly, solemnly, softly, over and over,
he makes known his presence,
his call a falling of mournful notes,
his tone much like the dove's.

To tell the truth,
I believe I could be happy
doing nothing but reading old diaries
morning to night. Silk and muslin
brush my hands like moths
passing by, the dancers
go up and down the room, no one
has learned the Valse as yet,
fiddle and flute and fortepiano
return to the older rhythms.
Birth and death, the fortunes of war,
fear and relief from fear
compel attention, yet
they're veiled in the mild Septembery
haze of time—blessedly present, blessedly
long gone by. Aware of the shame
I ought to feel—defecting
so willingly from my own century—
I stroll calmly through candlelit rooms
and down to the quay, to board
a waiting vessel that sails with the tide
into *the finest clear night*
possible, the Comet more beautiful
than anything I ever saw,
and the noise of the herrings,
which passed us
in immense shoals, glittering
in the Sea, like fire . . .

As the Moon Was Waning

Small intimations of destiny wove
a hammock about me out of fine
wiry fibers, a steel gossamer swaying
calmly in chaos. What I needed
was to examine it inch by inch,
discover it true or false, shelter or prison.
Instead, I lay low, evasive,
imagining mortal weariness that it's not yet time for.
Only the neighbor's new, very delicate, distant,
mercurial windbells promised,
if not tonight, then some night soon, to recall me
to that scrutiny, that obligation deferred—
as if their music,
sparse, random, uninsistent, nevertheless
would prove, in time,
a summons I'd not resist.

When the world comes to you muffled *as through a glass*
darkly—jubilance, anguish, declined into
faded postcards—remember how, seventeen, you said
you no longer felt or saw with the old
intensity, and knew that the flamelight
would not rekindle; and how Bet scoffed
and refused to believe you. And how many thousand times,
burning with joy or despair, you've known she was right.

Brown bird, irresolute as a dry
leaf, swerved in flight
just as my thought
changed course, as if I heard
a new motif enter a music I'd not
till then attended to.

Just when you seem to yourself
nothing but a flimsy web
of questions, you are given
the questions of others to hold
in the emptiness of your hands,
songbird eggs that can still hatch
if you keep them warm,
butterflies opening and closing themselves
in your cupped palms, trusting you not to injure
their scintillant fur, their dust.
You are given the questions of others
as if they were answers
to all you ask. Yes, perhaps
this gift is your answer.

Crow Spring

The crows are tossing themselves
recklessly in the random winds
of spring.
        One friend has died, one disappeared
    (for now, at least) leaving no address;
    I've lost the whereabouts
    of a wandering third. That seems to be,
    this year, the nature of this season.
    Is it a message about relinquishment?
Across the water, rain's veil, gray silk,
flattens the woods to two dimensions.
While close at hand
the crows' black fountain
jets and falls, jets and blows
this way and that.
How they scoop themselves
up from airy nadirs!

II
Sojourns in the Parallel World

They are going to
         daylight a river here—
that's what they call it, noun to verb.
A stream turned out
         years ago from its channel
to run in cement tunnels, dank and airless
         till it joined a sewer,
will be released—to sun, rain, pebbles, mud,
         yellow iris, the sky above it
and trees leaning over to be reflected!

At night, stars or at least streetlamps
         will gleam in it,
fish and waterbugs swim again in its ripples;
         and though its course,
more or less the old one it followed before its
         years of humiliation,
will pass near shops and the parking lot's
         glittering metallic desert, yet
this unhoped-for pardon will once more permit
         the stream to offer itself at last
to the lake, the lake will accept it, take it
         into itself,
the stream restored will become pure lake.

Where a fold of fog
briefly lifts by the headland,
it reveals a shoal of
wave-glitterings
imitating fish as the ocean
plays unobserved.

Expanse of gray, of silver.
Only this one rockstrewn
shallow bay singled out
to be luminous jade.
                    Its breakers
sing hard, sing loud, the sound
heard clear on the hilltop. Perhaps
the red-tailed hawk, swaying its flight
so much higher, hears it as well.

Hail, ricocheting off stone and cement, angrily
sprinkling its rock-salt among fallen
blossoms on earth's
half-awakened darkness,
                  enters
    the folds of sturdy camellias
    as if to seek
    refuge in those phyllo-layers of immaculate soft red,
    a place in which
                to come to rest,
                        to melt.

The 6:30 Bus, Late May

The mountain
a moonflower in late
blue afternoon.

The bus
grinds and growls.
At each stop

someone gets off,
the workday over,
heads for home.

Trees in their first
abundance of green
hold their breath,

the sky is
so quiet, cloudless.
The mountain

mutely
by arcane power
summons the moon.

All day the mountain boldly
displayed its white splendor,
disavowing all ambiguity,

but now, the long June day
just closing, the pale sky
still blue, the risen moon
well aloft, the mountain
retreats from so much pomp,
such flagrant and superficial pride,

and drifts above the horizon,
ghostly, irresolute, more akin
to a frail white moth

than to the massive tension
of rock, its own bones, beneath
its flesh of snow.

The Mountain Assailed

Animal mountain,
some of your snows are melting,
dark streaks reveal
your clefts, your secret creases.
The light quivers,
is it blue, is it gold?
I feel your breath
over the distance,
you are panting, the sun
gives you no respite.

Pentimento

To be discerned
        only by those
                alert to likelihood—

the mountain's form
        beneath the milky radiance
                which revokes it.

It lingers—
        a draft
            the artist may return to.

3 Short Solos

1

Softest of shadows
brave the mist, diluted gold
films the puddles.
Gingerly the sun
lowers itself
behind the hill of houses,
calling for evening:
it is only March, this day
has lasted long enough.

2

The red madrone's
undone by some unknown
disease. A robin
witlessly repeats among its branches
the old news, *spring,*
spring is begun.

3

Wickering from the lake, a bird
barely rising seems to ride
its own wake into air—only
to splash down nearby on the waveless water.

Pearblossom bright white
against green young leaves that frame
each tuft, black
pinewoods, graybrown buildings—

but rich
cream against strewn
feathers of cloud that float
slowly through new
blue of an April morning.

Rainbow Weather

The rain-curtains are blowing
north past the woods

and now the sun
looks out of its blue window

and they blow
right into a rainbow

arched above the lake
to see its own reflection

crinkled among the somber
festivities of fish!

Deep night, deep woods,
valley far below the steep
thigh of the hill, the sky too
a hazy darkness—yet the moon,
small and high, discovers
a wide stretch of river
to be its mirror, steel
brighter than its own
fogmuffled radiance.

Artery of ice,
winding sinuous down between
scarred hillsides, remnant
forests, clearcut raw
scraggy declivities. Above,
pale capillaries mark where,
when it thaws, this
frozen stream will take
the thin soil down with it.
Meanwhile it lies
white on gradations
of nuanced grey,
flowing to black, elegant design
to be acknowledged,
detached arabesque, a beauty
not to be denied.

What the spider weaves
is targets, dart-boards
of delicate design.
Flimsy prey, too insubstantial
to have a common name,
come blundering into them,
arrows each breeze
deflects from vague intentions.
Autumn raindrops adorn
the dead, the living,
the beauty of the web.
The entire arrangement
shakes and steadies, shakes
and steadies, complacent,
exquisite, efficient.

Rain-diamonds, this winter morning,
embellish the tangle of unpruned
pear-tree twigs; each solitaire,
placed, it appears, with considered
judgement, bears the light
beneath the rifted clouds—the indivisible
shared out in endless abundance.

When the light, late in the afternoon, pauses among
the highest branches of the highest trees,
they stir a little, as if in pleasure. Light and a passing breeze
become one and the same, a caress. Then the lower branches,
leaves or needles in shadow, take up the lilt
of that response, their green with its hint of blue forming
what, if it were sound, could be called
a chord with the almost yellow of those
the sunlight tarries with.

Stillness of flowers. Colors
a slow intense fire, faces
cool to the touch, burning.
Massed flowers in dusk, crimson,
magenta, orange,
unflickering furnace, gaze
unswerving, innocent scarlet,
ardent white, afloat
on late light, serene passion
stiller than silence.

Fish in the sky of water—silverly
as travelling moon through cloud-hills—
down current whisks, or deeper
fins into depths, to rise or sagely
wait in the milky mist of
disturbed sediment, wheeling briskly
at least whim, at one
with the aqueous everything it shines in.

The sea barely crinkled, breathing
calmly. Islands and shore
pure darkness, uncompromised,
outline and mass without
perplexity of component forms,
the salt grasses at water's edge
a frieze, immobile. All of this
a visible gravity,
not sad but serious.
                And above,
the light to which this somber peace
has not yet awoken, the sun
struggling to rise as one fights sometimes
to break out of fearful dreams
unable to shout or move—and clouds
in delicate brilliance sweeping
long aquiline curves, wild arabesques
across the east, drinking the rising
light, light, as it streams
out from that mortal struggle from which
the sun is already gasping free.

Island or dark
hollow of advancing wave?
Beyond
surf and spray a somber
horizontal. As if the sea
raised up
a sudden bulwark.
A menacing land, if land—
frowning escarpment, ephemeral
yet enduring, uncharted,
rumored. If wave,
a thundered prophetic word
in ocean's tongue, a bar of blackest
iron brandished aloft
in two fists of a water-god,
a warning not meant kindly.

Upon the darkish, thin, half-broken ice
there seemed to lie a barrel-sized, heart-shaped snowball,
frozen hard, its white
identical with the untrodden white
of the lake shore. Closer, its somber face—
mask and beak—came clear, the neck's
long cylinder, and the splayed feet, balanced,
weary, immobile. Black water traced, behind it,
an abandoned gesture. Soft
in still air, snowflakes
fell and fell. Silence
deepened, deepened. The short day
suspended itself, endless.

Almost too late to walk in the woods, but I did,
anyway. And stepping aside for a moment
from the shadowy path to enter
darker shadow, a favorite circle of fir trees,
received a gift from the dusk:

a small owl, not affrighted, merely
moving deliberately
to a branch a few feet
further from me, looked
full at me—a long regard,
steady, acknowledging, unbiassed.

A Wren

Quiet among the leaves, a wren,
fearless as if I were invisible
or moved with a silence like its own.

From bush to bush
it flies without hesitation,
no flutter or whirring of wings.
I feel myself lifted,
lightened, dispersed:

it has turned me to air,
it can fly right through me.

And again—after an absence
of months, first his, then mine—
when I return greyhearted
to the sunny shore, and find
St. Simon Heron has returned too:
that startled, glad
intake of breath, that sense
of blessing! Surely these sightings,
familiar but always
strange with unearned joy,
are a sign of covenant it's
grossly churlish to disregard. Heavily,
I begin to lift my wings.

One of my best encounters with animals
was meeting the ferret.
                            Stoats, weasels, ferrets
have evil reputations, and are indeed
without mercy (but has any creature but ourselves
even the potential for mercy
unless within its own species?
Rarely though we use it, amongst us or beyond,
we do have it, it's a human
distinguishing mark, like some colored
underwing feather or prehensile digit;
an offshoot of Imagination).
                            This ferret,
svelte, alert, but not long woken
from a daytime nap, showed, when it yawned,
those sharp little teeth that can draw from rabbits
the unforgettable scream they give with a last breath,
a scream filling the woods, echoing
down a listener's decades. But named, petted,
consenting to walk on a leash,
this ferret, out for a stroll
in the public park of a small town
somewhere in America,
came to my hands as if smiling, clambered
onto my shoulder, twined cosily
round my neck, rubbed noses with me.
I've never felt fur cloud-softer. I envied
the boy it lived with—I can't say 'owner,'
or 'tamer'—it seemed neither owned nor tamed
but a creature willing to try out
the Peaceable Kingdom: to just

47

begin it, without waiting.
                                    I knew
it was restless, nocturnal, demanding,
and wouldn't fit into my life. But I longed,
nevertheless, to have my own ferret.

Sojourns in the Parallel World

We live our lives of human passions,
cruelties, dreams, concepts,
crimes and the exercise of virtue
in and beside a world devoid
of our preoccupations, free
from apprehension—though affected,
certainly, by our actions. A world
parallel to our own though overlapping.
We call it 'Nature;' only reluctantly
admitting ourselves to be 'Nature' too.
Whenever we lose track of our own obsessions,
our self-concerns, because we drift for a minute,
an hour even, of pure (almost pure)
response to that insouciant life:
cloud, bird, fox, the flow of light, the dancing
pilgrimage of water, vast stillness
of spellbound ephemerae on a lit windowpane,
animal voices, mineral hum, wind
conversing with rain, ocean with rock, stuttering
of fire to coal—then something tethered
in us, hobbled like a donkey on its patch
of gnawed grass and thistles, breaks free.
No one discovers
just where we've been, when we're caught up again
into our own sphere (where we must
return, indeed, to evolve our destinies)
—but we have changed, a little.

III
It Should Be Visible

Protesting at the Nuclear Test Site

A year before, this desert
had raised its claws to me,
importunate and indifferent, half-naked beggar
displaying sores at the city gates.
Now again, in the raw glare
of Lent. Spikes, thorns, spines.
Where was the beauty others perceived?
I could not.
        But when the Shoshone elder spoke,
last year and now once more,
slowly I began to see what I saw as ugly were marks
of torture. When he was young this was desert, too,
but of different aspect, austere but joyful.
A people's reverence illumined stony ground.
Now, as my mind knew but imagination strained to acknowledge,
deep, deep and narrow the holes were bored
into the land's innards, and there, in savage routine,
Hiroshima blasts exploded, exploded, rape
repeated month after month for years.
What repelled me here was no common aridity
unappealing to lovers of lakes and trees,
but anguish, lineaments drab with anguish. This terrain
turned to the human world a gaze
of scorn, victim to tormentor.
        Slowly,
revulsion unstiffened itself, I learned
almost to love
the dry and hostile earth, its dusty growth
of low harsh plants, sparse in unceasing wind;
could almost have bent
to kiss that leper face.

The News and a Green Moon. July 1994.

The green moon, almost full.
Huge telescopes are trained on catastrophe:
comet fragments crash into Jupiter, gouging
craters gleeful astronomers say are bigger than Earth
(or profound displacements, others claim—tunnels, if you will—
in that planet's gaseous insubstantiality).

Visualize that. Visualize the News. The radio
has an hour to deliver so much. Cooperate.
Two thirds of what's left of Rwanda's people after the massacres
milling about in foodless, waterless camps.
Or not milling about, because they're dying

or dead. The green moon, or maybe
when it rises tomorrow in Rwanda or Zaire it will look
white, yellow, serenely silver. Here in the steamy gray
of heatwave dusk it's green as lime. Twenty five years ago
absurd figures, Michelin tire logos, bounced on the moon, whitely.

An audio report from Haiti: Voodoo believers
scrub themselves frantically under a waterfall,
wailing and shouting—you can hear the water behind them.
A purification ritual. Not a response to astronomical events
but to misery. Names change, the Tonton Macoute not mentioned

of late, but misery's tentacles don't relax. Babies now
(as the mike moves on), more wailing, no shouting, a hospital,
mothers and nuns sing hymns, there's not much food to give out.
Young men's bodies, hands tied behind them, litter the streets
of Port au Prince. (As rivers and lakes

in Africa have been littered recently, and not long ago in Salvador—
a familiar item of News.) The crowded boats (again) set out,
sink or are turned back. There could be, a scientist says
(the program returns to Jupiter) an untracked comet any time
heading for Earth. No way to stop it. Meanwhile

an aging astronaut says he regrets we're not sending men to Mars,
that would be progress, he thinks, a mild-mannered man, he thinks
too much has been spent on Welfare, all his devotion given to
    leaving
uncherished Earth behind, none to some one particular field or tree
and whatever knows it as home, none to the human past either,

certainly none to sacred mountains and wells or nontechnological
orders of knowledge. And meanwhile I'm reading Leonardo
    Sciascia's
furious refinements of ironic analysis, mirrored pathways
of the world's corruption in Sicily's microcosm. I feel the weight
of moral torpor; the old buoyant will for change that found me
    actions

to reflect itself (as the moon finds mirrors in seas and puddles)
butts its head on surfaces that give back no image. Slowly, one speck
to a square meter, cometary dust, continually as if from an
    inexhaustible
talcum shaker, falls unseen, adding century by century its increment
to Earth's burden. Covered in that unseen dust I'm peering up to
    see

the haze of green radiance the moon gives off this night, this one
    quick
breath of time. No lunamancy tells me its significance, if it has one.
It is beautiful, a beryl, a disk of soft jade melting
into its own light. So silent.
And earth's cries of anguish almost audible.

If from Space not only sapphire continents,
swirling oceans, were visible, but the wars—
like bonfires, wildfires, forest conflagrations,
flame and smoky smoulder—the Earth would seem
a bitter pomander ball bristling with poison cloves.
And each war fuelled with weapons: it should be visible
that great sums of money have been exchanged,
great profits made, workers gainfully employed
to construct destruction, national economies distorted
so that these fires, these wars, may burn
and consume the joy of this one planet
which, seen from outside its transparent tender shell,
is so serene, so fortunate, with its water, air
and myriad forms of 'life that wants to live.'
It should be visible that this bluegreen globe
suffers a canker which is devouring it.

Everything is threatened, but meanwhile
everything presents itself:
the trees, that day and night
steadily stand there, amassing
lifetimes and moss, the bushes
eager with buds sharp as green
pencil-points. Bark of cedar,
brown braids, bark of fir, deep-creviced,
winter sunlight favoring
here a sapling, there an ancient snag,
ferns, lichen. And the lake
always ready to change its skin
to match the sky's least inflection.
Everything answers the rollcall,
and even, as is the custom,
speaks for those that are gone.
—Clearly, beyond sound:
that revolutionary *'Presente!'*

IV
Anamnesis

The Sea Inland

Heather, bracken, the tall Scotch Firs.
There on the mountain, as the wind
came and went in the trees, she could hear
the sea. Closing her eyes she watched it
leaping upon the strand and slowly
returning into itself, tumbling the shingle with it,
to leap again, the over and over
rush, leap forward, and slow withdrawal.
And watched seaweed sway in the pools,
and stretches of wet sand reflect
a gleam of jade as the waves
poised before plunging.
All this she heard and saw on the mountain,
days when there was no school—
long before I was born—as I do now
under Douglas Firs in a western land
long after her death, my now, her then
intermingled as vision and sound
mingle, and what is fleeting and what remains
outside of time.

For years the dead
were the terrible weight of their absence,
the weight of what one had not put in their hands.
Rarely a visitation—dream or vision—
lifted that load for a moment, like someone
standing behind one and briefly taking
the heft of a frameless pack.
But the straps remained, and the ache—
though you can learn not to feel it
except when malicious memory
pulls downward with sudden force.
Slowly there comes a sense
that for some time the burden
has been what you need anyway.
How flimsy to be without it, ungrounded, blown
hither and thither, colliding with stern solids.
And then they begin to return, the dead:
but not as visions. They're not
separate now, not to be seen, no,
it's they who see: they displace,
for seconds, for minutes, maybe longer,
the mourner's gaze with their own. Just now,
that shift of light, arpeggio
on ocean's harp—
not the accustomed bearer
of heavy absence saw it, it was perceived
by the long-dead, long absent, looking
out from within one's wideopen eyes.

Sometimes I'd make of Valentines, long ago,
a wilder place than it was—
the sluice where a man-made lake spilled into Cranbrook
perceived as a cascade huge in mesmeric power:
I'd lean my arms on the 'rustic' fence
and gaze myself into almost-trance.
And now, leaving my sixth decade, I attribute sometimes
the freedom and shy charm of mountain rills in Wales
to the tiny stream that playfully
runs past the ponds at the hatchery, forming
miniature falls before, through stonework channels
built in the Thirties, it passes
under the road and joins the lake.
Viciously sentimental, this habit would be,
of vesting the commonplace in robes of glory
if I deceived myself a fraction more.
But even in childhood I knew
the difference, saw with a double vision.
And I've found the custom gives, in time,
new spirit to fact—or restores it. Places
reveal, as it were, their longings. Inherent dreams.
With the will to see
more than is there, one comes, at moments,
to perceive the more that there is:
from behind gray curtains of low expectation
it is drawn forth, resplendent.

You try to keep the present
        uppermost in your mind, counting its blessings
        (which today are many) because
although you are not without hope for the world, crazy
        as that seems to your gloomier friends and often
        to yourself, yet your own hopes
have shrunk, options are less abundant. Ages ago
        you enjoyed thinking of names
        for a daughter; later you still entertained,
at least as hypothesis, the notion
        of a not impossible love, requited passion;
        or resolved modestly to learn
some craft, various languages.
        And all those sparks of future
        winked out behind you, forgettable. So—
the present. Its blessings
        many today:
        the fresh, ornate
blossoms of the simplest trees a sudden
        irregular pattern everywhere, audacious white,
        flamingo pink in a haze of early warmth.
But perversely it's not
        what you crave. You want
        the past. Oh, not your own,
no reliving of anything—no, what you hanker after
        is a compost,
        a forest floor, thick, saturate,
fathoms deep, palimpsestuous, its surface a mosaic
        of infinitely fragile, lacy, tenacious
        skeleton leaves. When you put your ear
to that odorous ground you can catch the unmusical, undefeated
        belling note, as of a wounded stag escaped triumphant,
        of lives long gone.

Sheep in the Weeds

Simmer and drowse of August. And the sheep
single file
threading a wavering path, because
the mood takes them, or took
the bellwether, to go
this way, not that,
the length of the long field.
Coarse grass,
a powdery green. Hum
of bees, heat of noon
among seeding thistles. Silver,
purple.

Almost bodily
something returns,
a heavy
note or two of sensual music.
A moment
of milkweed sweetness
long past,

a river
unseen beyond
the field's vague edge.

Without nostalgia,
a neutral
timelessness. Its shadow,
still tight as skin around it,
rehearses in silence
the message
it will deliver later,
about time.

The London Plane

"Xerxes' *strange* Lydian *love,*
the Platane *tree."*
John Donne, 'The Autumnal'

Primrose dapple on grey. Majestic
trunk and limbs, and then
the toy-like bobbles among the tangle
of small branches, random twigs.
Strange Lydian love, you evoke, anywhere,
the old streets of my city, forever filled
with promise and history.

Anamnesis at the Faultline

For Barbara Thomas, after
experiencing her installation,
"What is Found, What is Lost, What
Is Remembered," 1992

I

In each house, imprinted,
a journey.   Partings, tearings
                              apart: storm, loss, hands
                              upraised for rescue,
                              onrush of wave,
                              exile.
Long-hidden, the time
of arrival, plumb-line,
first foundation.

How does memory
serve, serve the earth?
                              Columns
                              of turned wood placed
                              among broken stones,
                              perches for companion
                              ravens. A way
                              of witness.

II

House, hill-field, open
shell of stillness:
                              passage
                              through
                              from doorless
                              doorway
                              to doorway
                              to sky.

The wind
     where it listeth.

III

In each bird,
storm-voyage.

In each tilted
cross, human
dreams,
clouds,
the shifting
seasons.

And in each grave.

     In each stasis,
     impetus. Dark
     edifice, backlit, bigger
     than house or grave. White
     gold of its aura.

Complaint and Rejoinder

There's a kind of despair, when your friends
are scattered across the world; you see
how therefore never is there a way
each can envision truly
the others of whom you speak.
                    Oceans divide your life,
you want to place all of it—
people, places, their tones, atmospheres,
everything shared uniquely with each—
into a single bowl, like petals, like sand
in a pail. No one can ever hear or tell
the whole story.

(And do you really think
this would not be so if you lived
all of your life on an island,
in a village too small to contain
a single stranger?)

My friendships with one to two, yes, three
men for whom once I felt
the wildest, most painful longing,
still retain, in their enduring transformation,
some fragrance of those times,
like a box where once
the leaves of an exotic herb were kept,
an herb of varied properties, useful and dangerous,
long since consumed.

The Great Black Heron

Since I stroll in the woods more often
than on this frequented path, it's usually
trees I observe; but among fellow humans
what I like best is to see an old woman
fishing alone at the end of a jetty,
hours on end, plainly content.
The Russians mushroom-hunting after a rain
trail after themselves a world of red sarafans,
nightingales, samovars, stoves to sleep on
(though without doubt those are not
what they can remember). Vietnamese families
fishing or simply sitting as close as they can
to the water, make me recall that lake in Hanoi
in the amber light, our first, jet-lagged evening,
peace in the war we had come to witness.
This woman engaged in her pleasure evokes
an entire culture, tenacious field-flower
growing itself among rows of cotton
in red-earth country, under the feet
of mules and masters. I see her
a barefoot child by a muddy river
learning her skill with the pole. What battles
has she survived, what labors?
She's gathered up all the time in the world
—nothing else—and waits for scanty trophies,
complete in herself as a heron.

My father's serviette ring,
silver incised with a design
of Scotch thistles, the central medallion
uninitialled, a blank oval.
                              The two massive
German kitchen knives, pre-1914, not-stainless steel,
which my mother carefully scoured with Vim
after each use.
                    My daily use
of these and other such things
links me to hands long gone.

Medieval con-men disgust and amuse us,
we think we'd never have fallen
for such crude deceptions—unholy
animal bones, nails from any old barn,
splinters enough from the Cross to fill
a whole lumber-yard.
                          But can we
with decency mock the gullible
for desiring these things?
                              Who doesn't want
to hold what hands belov'd or venerated
were accustomed to hold?—You? I?
                              who wouldn't want
to put their lips to the true chalice?

The morning after your midnight death
I wake to Lieder—
Schumann, Schubert, the Goethe settings.
Why did I not make sure that you
(and your partner also before his death,
whose cabaret songs would perhaps
have pleased Franz Schubert) came to know
this music?
        This is the way
mourning always begins to take root
and add itself to one's life. A new
pearl-grey thread entering the weave:
this longing to show, to share,
which runs full tilt into absence.

Southwest the moon
full and clear,

eastward, the sky
reddening, cloudless
over fir trees, the dark hill.

I remember, decades ago,
'day coming and the moon not gone,'
the low ridge of the Luberon
beyond the well

and Ste. Victoire
shifting its planes and angles
yet again.

V
Representations

Representations

Daybreak

A winding uphill road. The valley still
deep in shadow. Sunlight
scales the mountain, reaches in
to towers, pinnacles—a city
transformed by daybreak and distance.
Larger than life, a human figure
backlit by the dazzle. Black and white,
but we see it as gold, we see it
as gold and silver.

Pilgrims

Pilgrims among the dune-grass, returning
to their small beached boat. Hurry,
or else the tide will lift it
to drift out to sea! They stumble
in soft sand tufted
with starry flowers.

Seeing the Unseen

Snow, large flakes,
whirling in midnight air,
unseen, coming to rest
on a fast-asleep, very small village
set among rocky fields; not one
lit square of wakeful window.

He silent and angry,
she silent and afraid, each looking
out the cab windows,
he to the left, she to the right,
both dressed for winter, driving
somewhere neither wants to go.

Moongaze

Full moon's unequivocal
curious stare: the palm-trees
range their lanky shadows defiantly
on the sand for inspection,
motionless as resting spiders.

Alleluia

Angels carved from oak surround
the empty tomb, holding
the hammer and nails, the dice,
the crown of rose-thorns. Mute air
of bitter praises in their singing mouths.
What sharp-ridged wings, what shine
of oaken feathers!

Station of Solitude

Alone in his tiny station, the platform latticed with shadows
that tell us a simple fencelike gate is behind him,
shut at the level crossing, the stationmaster watches
the train slowly grow larger. The signal is ready.
Puffing and clanging, *forte, fortissimo:*

a second to go, and it's here—
the first event of the day.
                    There's a single track.
At dusk, when the whitish sky consents
to be briefly brilliant, he'll watch the same train dwindle
back up the line, curve into distance; and silence,
complacently, like a cat dislodged yet again
from its place by the hearth, will reoccupy all the air.
He'll furl the redundant flag. The second event
will be over. That's all. No express
with its scream of triumph, its flash
of glittering windows, of rosy-shaded dining-car lamps
ever passed this way, ever will.

                                        Male Voice Choir

They move from left to right on the road below,
a column of Russian soldiers marching or being marched
to the onion-domed church for Sunday liturgy, sergeant
bringing up the rear, officer on horseback leading,
none of them welcome here
in Poland, 1910.
                    From a grassy bank
the bride from a distant country, resting
in summer sun, watches, and later sees them return,
shriven and springy, swinging their arms, singing.
Hearing the basses, mineshaft deep,
the altos climbing like larks,
the folksong's yearning, the merry sudden
accelerations, a dance of voices, she remembers
the colliers practicing for an Eisteddfod, twilights of summer,
her childhood village.
                    A free afternoon is stretching
before the Tzar's mouzhik conscripts, prospect
of vodka and sleep. They are far from home.
                                        She holds

79

her husband's hand, warm, smooth, and safe.
But there are tears on her cheeks, the live coals
of such harmonies brand her heart.

Time Retrieved

It is late in a mild English autumn. All of the leaves
have fallen, and now (the now of the eighteen eighties,
eternal) lie in the long trafficless road that leads
away into fields, past the lit windows of one last
large building, a school or seminary. One figure
servant or seamstress, quietly recedes from us, scarcely
rustling the pavement leaves, carrying a basket; she's gazing
over a garden wall to the source of the lemony glow tinting
a sky cloudless yet faintly bonfire-smoky: the sun
is just now dipping below the woods she can see
though we can ony deduce their branchy darkness
from these roadside trees, so black, so confident
in their stripped beauty, intricate logic of twigs. A wall
across the street encloses the grounds
of an unseen house; wiry strands of a bare vine
interlace themselves with pale twig-shadow—the fading gold
still almost red on the bricks. From the russet carpet
up through the muffled tawny low horizon
to the transparent muted yellow above,
which is almost already
tinged with the wistful green it may hold
for a minute or two before dark, that glow
suffuses all, it touches the girl's cheek
just seen as she moves homeward, and the edge of her cap,
and the closed door to the hidden garden.

VI
Raga

The Visual Element

Feet moving only to shift weight, the conductor
dances, an old bamboo leaning
a flexible torso into the gusting music,
precisely waving, uttering choreographically
the song the orchestra
makes audible.

String players barely glance his way,
long since linked to him
by unseen strands of spider-silk;
bows move in unison,
like wheat stirred in the wind's
rhythmic passing.
And wind-players glance
left and right, secretly watchful
like small animals. Twitch of an eyebrow:
silent appoggiatura.

Violinist, alone as on a martyr's cross,
you have forgotten us.
It's not always this way,
I've seen plenty of others playing
the audience along with the music;
but you, exposed, tortured, ecstatic—
should we not close our eyes?
Have we the right to perceive
the blindness of you, your white face,
badly tailored suit, awkward stance
and deeply erotic abandon, as well as to accept
this intricate energy, this weight, this outpouring
of light which Bach
permits you to suffer, permits you to offer?

Angel with heavy wings
weathering the stormwracked air,
listing heavenward.

Intervals
so frank,
open and major as you like,
rhythms
a child could keep—

only Haydn dared
make magic from such
morning suns,
roadside gold, each dandelion
dipped in his elixir,
the secret depths of candor.

The golden brushwood! But that
says nothing to you. Think perhaps
of strokes calligraphic yet delineatory,
sepia, the ground grayish,
a subtle wrist guiding
the rather dry brush—it turns,
lifts.
    And then
recollection of bells, one moment only.
And moving on. Moving
along the brief path, charged
with still unlit brands that will gild the dark.

The fluteplayer
can't be seen to draw breath,
doesn't even
part his lips. But music
flows from the
wooden flute, a river
of honey over–
flowing the honeycomb.

VII
A South Wind

Looking, Walking, Being

*"The world is not something to
look at, it is something to be in."*
Mark Rudman

I look and look.
Looking's a way of being: one becomes,
sometimes, a pair of eyes walking.
Walking wherever looking takes one.

The eyes
dig and burrow into the world.
They touch
fanfare, howl, madrigal, clamor.
World and the past of it,
not only
visible present, solid and shadow
that looks at one looking.

And language? Rhythms
of echo and interruption?
That's
a way of breathing,

breathing to sustain
looking,
walking and looking,
through the world,
in it.

Short grass, electric green, the ground
soggy from winter rain, Chaucerian
eyes of day, minute petals rose-tinted,
nourished by droppings of ducks and geese.
Hold fast what seem ephemera—
plain details that rise clear
beyond the fog of half-thoughts,
that rustling static, empty of metaphor.
Nothing much, or everything; all depends
on how you regard it.
                    On *if* you regard it.
                                Note the chalk–
yellow of hazel catkins, how in the wet
mild wind they swing toward spring.

The Lyre-Tree

There was a dead tree in the woods
whose two remaining limbs sprang upward
in semblance of a lyre.
                    And now
one has snapped off. What remains
cannot signify.
              O Orpheus,
lend me power to sing
the unheard music of that vanished lyre.

They speak of bonding. Of the infant, the primitive
without sense of boundary, everything as much
or as little itself as itself.

                                        Yet what loneliness,
the solitude
of thought before language. A kind of darkness
stirring the mind, blurring
the glare and glitter of vision,
steam on the white mirror.

Primal Speech

If there's an Ur-language still among us,
hiding out like a pygmy pterodactyl
in the woods, sighted at daybreak sometimes,
perched on a telephone wire, or like
prehistoric fish discovered in ocean's
deepest grottoes, then it's the exclamation,
universal whatever the sound, the triumphant,
wondering, infant utterance, 'This! This!',
showing and proffering the thing, anything,
the affirmation even before the naming.

For Those Whom the Gods Love Less

When you discover
your new work travels the ground you had traversed
decades ago, you wonder, panicked,
'Have I outlived my vocation? Said already
all that was mine to say?'
                              There's a remedy—
only one—for the paralysis seizing your throat to mute you,
numbing your hands: Remember the great ones, remember
    Cezanne
doggedly *sur le motif*, his mountain
a tireless noonday angel he grappled like Jacob,
demanding reluctant blessing. Remember James rehearsing
over and over his theme, the loss
of innocence and the attainment
(note by separate note sounding its tone
until by accretion a chord resounds) of somber
understanding. Each life in art
goes forth to meet dragons that rise from their bloody scales
in cyclic rhythm: Know and forget, know and forget.
It's not only
the passion for *getting it right* (though it's that, too)
it's the way
radiant epiphanies recur, recur,
consuming, pristine, unrecognized—
until remembrance dismays you. And then, look,
some inflection of light, some wing of shadow
is other, unvoiced. You can, you must
proceed.

The Hymn

Had I died, or was I
very old and blind, or
was the dream—
this hymn, this ecstatic paean,
this woven music
of color and form, of the sense
of airy space—
was the dream
showing forth the power
of Memory, now, today or at any
moment of need? Or the power
of the inner eye, distinct
from Memory, Imagination's power,
greater than we remember,
in abeyance, the well in which
we forget to dip our cups?

At all events,
that broad hillside of trees
all in leaf, trees of all kinds,
all hues of green, gold-greens, blue-greens,
black-greens, pure and essential
green-greens, and warm and deep
maroons, too, and the almost purple
of smoketrees—all perceived
in their mass of rounded, composed forms
across a half mile of breezy air,
yet with each leaf
rippling, gleaming,
visible almost to vein and serration:

at all events, that sight
brought with it, in dream
such gladness, I wept
tears of gratitude

(such as I've never wept, only read
that such tears sometimes
are shed) amazed to know
this power was mine, a thing given,
to see so well, though asleep,
though blind,
though gone from the earth.

Writer and Reader

When a poem has come to me,
almost complete as it makes its way
into daylight, out through arm, hand, pen,
onto page; or needing
draft after draft, the increments
of change toward itself, what's missing
brought to it, grafted
into it, trammels of excess
peeled away till it can breathe
and leave me—

then I feel awe at being
chosen for the task
again; and delight, and the strange and familiar
sense of destiny.

But when I read or hear
a perfect poem, brought into being
by someone else, someone perhaps
I've never heard of before—a poem
bringing me pristine visions, music
beyond what I thought I could hear,
a stirring, a leaping
of new anguish, of new hope, a poem
trembling with its own
vital power—

then I'm caught up beyond
that isolate awe, that narrow delight,
into what singers must feel in a great choir,
each with humility and zest partaking
of harmonies they combine to make,

waves and ripples of music's ocean,
who hush to listen when the aria
arches above them in halcyon stillness.

Your Heron

for Ben Saenz

From stillness
the Great Blue Heron
rose without warning,

winged in robust decision
up and across
the sky-filled water.

You shared
the unfailing joy of it,
we laughed in pleasure.

Later the heron
turned white in your mind,
conflated with egrets.

Memory and dream, joined in Imagination's
'esemplastic power,' gave you the great
winged symbol, rising

or plummeting, as the creative
work required, experience feeding
the mind's vision, that moves

with beating wings
into and over
the page, the parable.

Beauty growls from the fertile dark.
Don't disturb
the glow. Shadows
are not contrivances devised
for your confusion. They grow
in subtle simplicity from the root,
silence.

    And words put forth
before there's time to hesitate about
their strangeness, are swaying bridges
(quick! You're across) to further
dark illumination,
lovely tarnish of old silver,
bronze long-buried.

        •

Alders crowd to the pool's edge.
From roots and bark seeps down
their dark spirit,
a gift to the water that assuages
their thirst. It dyes
the pool to a blacker depth,
a clarity
deeper and less apparent.

        •

Imagine the down of black swans.
Hidden beneath the smooth layers
of black breast-feathers, preened by red beaks,

That's the tender dark of certain nights
in summer, when the moon's away,
stars invisible over the moist
low roof of fog.
How good it would be to spend such a night
wholly attentive to its obscurity,
without thought of history, of words like
Dark Ages, Enlightment, or especially
Contemporary, the shameful news each day.
Wholly present to the beneficent
swansdown grace of a single night,
unlit by even a candle.

VIII
Close to a Lake

'In Whom We Live and Move and Have Our Being'

Birds afloat in air's current,
sacred breath? No, not breath of God,
it seems, but God
the air enveloping the whole
globe of being.
It's we who breathe, in, out, in, the sacred,
leaves astir, our wings
rising, ruffled—but only the saints
take flight. We cower
in cliff-crevice or edge out gingerly
on branches close to the nest. The wind
marks the passage of holy ones riding
that ocean of air. Slowly their wake
reaches us, rocks us.
But storm or still,
numb or poised in attention,
we inhale, exhale, inhale,
encompassed, encompassed.

What One Receives from Living Close to a Lake

That it is wide,
and still—yet subtly
stirring; wide and
level, reflecting the intangible sky's
vaster breadth in its own
fresh, cold, serene
surface we can
touch, enter, taste.
That it is wide
and uninterrupted save by
here a sail, there
a constellation of waterfowl—
a meadow of water
you could say,
a clearing amid the entangled
forest of forms and voices,
anxious intentions, urgent
memories: a deep, clear
breath to fill
the soul, an internal
gesture, arms
flung wide to echo
that mute
generous outstretching
we call *lake*.

The Beginning of Wisdom

Proverbs 9.–10

You have brought me so far.

•

I know so much. Names, verbs, images. My mind
overflows, a drawer that can't close.

•

Unscathed among the tortured. Ignorant parchment
uninscribed, light strokes only, where a scribe
tried out a pen.

•

I am so small, a speck of dust
moving across the huge world. The world
a speck of dust in the universe.

•

Are you holding
the universe? You hold
onto my smallness. How do you grasp it,
how does it not
slip away?

•

I know so little.

•

You have brought me so far.

'Straight to the point'
      can ricochet,
            unconvincing.
Circumlocution, analogy,
      parable's ambiguities, provide
            context, stepping-stones.

Most of the time. And then

the lightning power
      amidst these indirections,
            of plain
unheralded miracle!
      For example,
            as if forgetting
to prepare them, He simply
      walks on water
            toward them, casually—
and impetuous Peter, empowered,
      jumps from the boat and rushes
            on wave-tip to meet Him—
a few steps, anyway—
      (till it occurs to him,
            'I can't, this is preposterous'
and Jesus has to grab him,
      tumble his weight
            back over the gunwale).
Sustaining those light and swift
      steps was more than Peter
            could manage. Still,
years later,
      his toes and insteps, just before sleep,
            would remember their passage.

Conversion of Brother Lawrence

*'Let us enter into
ourselves, Time
presses.'*
Brother Lawrence
1611–1691

1

What leafless tree plunging
into what pent sky was it
convinced you Spring, bound to return
in all its unlikelihood, was a word
of God, a Divine message?
Custom, natural reason, are everyone's assurance;
we take the daylight for granted, the moon,
the measured tides. A particular tree, though,
one day in your eighteenth winter,
said more, an oracle. Clumsy footman,
apt to drop the ornate objects handed to you,
cursed and cuffed by butlers and grooms,
your inner life unsuspected,
you heard, that day, a more-than-green
voice from the stripped branches.
Wooden lace, a celestial geometry, uttered
more than familiar rhythms of growth.
It said *By the Grace of God.*
Midsummer rustled around you that wintry moment.
Was it elm, ash, poplar, a fruit-tree, your rooted
twig-winged angel of annunciation?

2

Out from the chateau park it sent you
(by some back lane, no doubt,
not through the wide gates of curled iron),

by ways untold, by soldier's marches, to the obscure
clatter and heat of a monastery kitchen,
a broom's rhythmic whisper for music,
your torment the drudgery of household ledgers. Destiny
without visible glory. 'Time pressed.' Among pots and pans,
heart-still through the bustle of chores,
your labors, hard as the pain in your lame leg,
grew slowly easier over the years, the years
when, though your soul felt darkened, heavy, worthless,
yet God, you discovered, never abandoned you but walked
at your side keeping pace as comrades had
on the long hard roads of war. You entered then
the unending 'silent secret conversation',
the life of steadfast attention.
Not work transformed you; work, even drudgery,
was transformed: that discourse
pierced through its monotones, infused them
with streams of sparkling color.
What needed doing, you did; journeyed if need be
on rocking boats, lame though you were,
to the vineyard country to purchase the year's wine
for a hundred Brothers, laughably rolling yourself
over the deck-stacked barrels when you couldn't
keep your footing; and managed deals with the vintners
to your own surprise, though business was nothing to you.
Your secret was not the craftsman's delight in process,
which doesn't distinguish work from pleasure—
your way was not to exalt nor avoid
the Adamic legacy, you simply made it irrelevant:
everything faded, thinned to nothing, beside
the light which bathed and warmed, the Presence
your being had opened to. Where it shone,

there life was, and abundantly; it touched
your dullest task, and the task was easy.
                    Joyful, absorbed,
you 'practiced the presence of God' as a musician
practices hour after hour his art:
'A stone before the carver,'
you 'entered into yourself.'

Dom Helder, octagenarian wisp
of human substance arrived from Brazil,
raises his arms and gazes toward
a sky pallid with heat, to implore
'Peace!'
        —then waves a 'goodbye for now'
to God, as to a *compadre*.
'The Mass is over, go in peace
to love and serve the Lord': he walks
down with the rest of us to cross
the cattle-grid, entering forbidden ground
where marshals wait with their handcuffs.

After hours of waiting,
penned into two wire-fenced enclosures, sun
climbing to cloudless zenith, till everyone
has been processed, booked, released to trudge
one by one up the slope to the boundary line
back to a freedom that's not so free,
we are all reassembled. We form
two circles, one contained in the other, to dance
clockwise and counterclockwise
like children in Duncan's vision.
But not to the song of ashes, of falling:
we dance in the unity that brought us here,
instinct pulls us into the ancient
rotation, symbol of continuance.
Light and persistent as tumbleweed,
but not adrift, Dom Helder, too,
faithful pilgrim, dances,
dances at the turning core.

On Belief in the Physical Resurrection of Jesus

It is for all
          'literalists of the imagination,'
                    poets or not,
that miracle
          is possible,
                    possible and essential.
Are some intricate minds
                    nourished
                              on concept,
as epiphytes flourish
                    high in the canopy?
                              Can they
subsist on the light,
                    on the half
                              of metaphor that's not
grounded in dust, grit,
                    heavy
                              carnal clay?
Do signs contain and utter,
                    for them
                              all the reality
that they need? Resurrection, for them,
                    an internal power, but not
                              a matter of flesh?
For the others,
          of whom I am one,
                    miracles (ultimate need, bread
of life) are miracles just because
                    people so tuned
                              to the humdrum laws:
gravity, mortality—
                    can't open
                              to symbol's power

unless convinced of its ground,
                                    its roots
                                            in bone and blood.
We must feel
              the pulse in the wound
                                        to believe
that 'with God
              all things
                        are possible,'
taste
      bread at Emmaus
                        that warm hands
broke and blessed.

Psalm Fragments (Schnittke String Trio)

This clinging to a God
for whom one does
nothing.
        A loyalty
without deeds.

.

           Tyrant God.
           Cruel God.
           Heartless God.

           God who permits
           the endless outrage we call
           History.

           Deaf God.
           Blind God.
           Idiot God.

           (Scapegoat god. Finally
           running out of accusations
           we deny Your existence.)

.

I don't forget
that downhill street
of spilled garbage and beat-up cars,
the gray faces
looking up, all color
gone with the sun—

disconsolate, prosaic twilight
at midday. And the fear
of blindness.

It's harder to recall
the relief when plain
daylight returned

subtly, softly,
without the fuss
of trumpets.
                    Yet
our faces had been upturned
like those of gazers
into a sky of angels
at Birth or Ascension.

                    •

Lord, I curl in Thy grey
gossamer hammock

that swings by one
elastic thread to thin
twigs that could, that should
break but don't.

          •

I do nothing, I give You
nothing. Yet You hold me

minute by minute
from falling.

Lord, You provide

The Prayer Plant (*Maranta Leuconeura*)

The prayer plant must long
for darkness, that it may fold and raise
its many pairs of green hands
to speak at last, in that gesture;

the way a shy believer,
at last in solitude, at last,
with what relief
kneels down to praise You.

The hand that inscribed Genesis left out
the creation of Time. Dividing
darkness from light, God paused to reach
into the substance of Eternity,
teased out a strand of it,
and wound its arabesques throughout
the workshop of creation, looping it through
the arches of newmade days and nights,
pulling and stretching each of them into aeons.
Our own lifetimes and centuries
were formed from leftover
bits and pieces, frayed
ends of God's ribbon, rags
from the Eternal scrapbag.

A Heresy

When God makes dust of our cooling magma,
musingly crumbling the last
galls and studs of our being,

the only place we can go if we're not
destined for hell, or there already,
is purgatory—for certainly heaven's
no place for a film of dust to settle;

and I see no reason why purgatory
may not be reincarnation, the soul
passing from human to another
earth-form more innocent—even to try

the human again, ablaze
with outsetting infant wonder—from which
to learn, as expiation progressed,
neglected tasks.
              Then

the sifting again, between thoughtful fingers,
the rubbing to finer substance.
                          Then perhaps
time for the floating
              into light,
                    to rest suspended
                    mote by silvery mote
              in that bright veil to await
the common resurrection.

Hovering light embraces
the yellowing poplars, four spires
evenly spaced, a dozen clustered
apart, all of them backed by foresty dark,
a curtain of conifers.

Waking and sleeping, there was grace, reassurance,
during the hours of darkness:
a change in perception, such as we read of
in 19th-century stories, when someone in fever
visibly passed from danger into a calm lagoon
of slumber, promising health.

The light on the trees a nimbus now
of downy yellow, embrace without pressure of weight,
compassionate light.

A Yellow Tulip

The yellow tulip in the room's warmth
opens.
Can I say it, and not seem to taunt
all who live in torment? Believe it, yet
remain aware of the world's anguish?
But it's so: a caravan arrives constantly
out of desert dust, laden
with gift beyond gift, beyond reason.
       Item: a yellow tulip
       opens; at its center
       a star of greenish indigo,
       a subtle wash of ink
       at the base of each of
       six large petals.
       The black stamens
       are dotted with white.
       At the core, the ovary,
       applegreen fullness
       tapering to proffer—sheltered
       in the wide cup of primary
       yellow—its triune stigma, clove
       of green and gold.
That's one, at nightfall of a day which brought
a dozen treasures, exotic surprises, landscapes,
music, words, acts of friendship, all of them wrapped
in mysterious silk, each unique.
How is it possible?
The yellow tulip
              in the room's warmth
                            opens.

The golden particles
descend, descend,
traverse the water's
depth and come to rest
on the level bed
of the well until,
the full descent
accomplished, water's
absolute transparence
is complete, unclouded
by constellations
of bright sand.
Is this
the place where you
are brought in meditation?
Transparency
seen for itself—
as if its quality
were not, after all,
to enable
perception *not* of itself?
With a wand
of willow I again
trouble the envisioned pool,
the cloudy nebulae
form and disperse,
the separate
grains again
slowly, slowly
perform their descent,
and again
stillness ensues,

and the mystery
of that sheer
clarity, is it water indeed,
or air, or light?

1

Again before your altar, silent Lord.
And here the sound of rushing waters,
a dove's crooning.

Not every temple serves
as your resting-place.
Here, though, today,
over the river's continuo,
under the dove's soliloquy,
your hospitable silence.

2

Again before thy altar, silent Lord.

Thy presence is made known
by untraced interventions
like those legendary baskets filled
with bread and wine, discovered
at the door by someone at wit's end
returning home empty-handed
after a day of looking for work.

To Live in the Mercy of God

To lie back under the tallest
oldest trees. How far the stems
rise, rise
      before ribs of shelter
            open!

To live in the mercy of God. The complete
sentence too adequate, has no give.
Awe, not comfort. Stone, elbows of
stony wood beneath lenient
moss bed.

And awe suddenly
passing beyond itself. Becomes
a form of comfort.
           Becomes the steady
     air you glide on, arms
stretched like the wings of flying foxes.
To hear the multiple silence
of trees, the rainy
forest depths of their listening.

To float, upheld,
     as salt water
     would hold you,
            once you dared.

   •

To live in the mercy of God.

To feel vibrate the enraptured

waterfall flinging itself
unabating down and down
                        to clenched fists of rock.
Swiftness of plunge,
hour after year after century,
                        O or Ah
uninterrupted, voice
many-stranded.
                        To breathe
spray. The smoke of it.
                        Arcs
of steelwhite foam, glissades
of fugitive jade barely perceptible. Such passion—
rage or joy?
                        Thus, not mild, not temperate,
God's love for the world. Vast
flood of mercy
                        flung on resistance.

Primary Wonder

Days pass when I forget the mystery.
Problems insoluble and problems offering
their own ignored solutions
jostle for my attention, they crowd its antechamber
along with a host of diversions, my courtiers, wearing
their colored clothes; cap and bells.
                                        And then
once more the quiet mystery
is present to me, the throng's clamor
recedes: the mystery
that there is anything, anything at all,
let alone cosmos, joy, memory, everything,
rather than void: and that, O Lord,
Creator, Hallowed One, You still,
hour by hour sustain it.

Notes

PAGE

14   'The Glittering Noise.' The italicized lines are quoted from *The Wynne Diaries 1789–1820*, edited by Anne Fremantle (Oxford University Press, 1935).

34, 35,   'Alchemy,' 'Double Vision,' 'Firmament,' 'Agon,' 'Warning,' 'Swan
40, 41,   in Falling Snow,' and 'Sheep in the Weeds.' From photographs by
42, 43,   Mary Randlett.
and 65

56   'It Should Be Visible.' The allusion is to Schweitzer's phrase: 'I am life that wants to live, among other lives that want to live.'

101   'Your Heron.' 'Esemplastic power': Coleridge's term.

111   'Conversion of Brother Lawrence.' The quotations are from Brother Lawrence's 'The Practice of the Presence of God' available in many editions), and the biographical allusions are based on the original introduction.

INDEX OF TITLES & FIRST LINES

134